Claude Lévi-Strauss
What's in a Name

ERIS
gems

TO SUM UP: BIRDS AND DOGS ARE relevant in connection with human society either because they suggest it by their own social life (which men look on as an imitation of theirs), or alternatively because having no social life of their own, they form part of ours.

Cattle, like dogs, form part of human society but as it were, asocially, since they verge on objects. Finally racehorses, like birds form a series disjoined from human society, but like cattle, lacking in intrinsic sociability.

If, therefore, birds are *metaphorical human beings* and dogs, *metonymical human beings*, cattle may be thought of as *metonymical inhuman beings* and racehorses as *metaphorical inhuman beings*. Cattle are contiguous only for want of similarity, racehorses similar only for want of contiguity. Each of these two categories offers the converse image of one of the two other categories, which themselves stand in the relation of inverted symmetry.

The linguistic equivalent of this system of psycho-sociological differences is to be found on the plane of appellations. Bird and dog names are derived from language. But, although they have the same paradigmatic character, they differ in that the former are real, while the latter are conventional christian names. The names of birds are taken from the preserve of ordinary human christian names, of which they constitute a part; while the names of dogs in effect reproduce in its entirety a portion of names formally similar to human christian names although rarely borne by ordinary human beings.

The names of cattle and horses derive rather from speech, since they are in both cases taken from the syntagmatic chain. But the names of cattle remain closest to it for, as descriptive terms, they are scarcely proper names. A cow habitually said to be gentle ('douce') is called 'Douce'. The names given to cattle thus survive as testimony of a bygone discourse, and they can at any moment resume their function of epithets in discourse: even when one talks to cattle, their character as objects never allows them to be anything but *what is spoken about*. The names of racehorses are 'within discourse' in a different fashion: not 'still in discourse' but 'made of discourse'. To find horses' names it is necessary to take the syntagmatic chain to pieces and to transform its discrete units into proper names which will not be able to figure in discourse in any other capacity unless the ambiguity is dispelled by the context. The difference here is due to the fact that cattle are ranked in the inhuman part of human society, while racehorses (who, objectively speaking, belong to the same category) primarily present the image of an antisociety to a restricted society which owes its existence entirely to them. The system of naming applied to them is the most frankly inhuman of all and the technique of linguistic demolition employed to construct it likewise the most barbarous.

When all is said and done, we arrive at a three-dimensional system. The upper line on the horizontal plane corresponds to the positive or negative metaphorical relation between human and animal society (birds) or between the society of men and the anti-society of horses, and the lower to the metonymical relation between the society of men on the one hand and dogs and cattle on the other which are members of the former in the capacity either of subjects or of objects.

The left-hand column on the vertical plane associates birds and dogs which have a metaphorical or a metonymical relation with social life. The right-hand column associates horses and cattle, which have no relation with social life, although cattle form part of it (metonymy) and racehorses bear a negative resemblance to it (metaphor).

Finally, two oblique axes have to be added, for the names given to birds and cattle are formed by metonymical appropriation (either from a paradigmatic set or from a syntagmatic chain), while the names given to dogs and horses are formed by metaphorical reproduction (either of a paradigmatic set or of a syntagmatic chain). What we have here is therefore a coherent system. The systematic relations between these usages are not their only interesting feature from our point of view. Although borrowed from our civilization where their place is a minor one, they offer ready access to other usages which are given extreme importance by the societies which employ them. The attention we have paid to certain aspects of our customs which some may consider futile is justified for two reasons. In the first place, we hope thereby to gain a clearer and more general idea of the nature of proper names. Secondly and above all, we are led to inquire into the hidden motives underlying ethnographic curiosity: the fascination exercised over us by customs apparently far removed from ours, the contradictory feeling of proximity and strangeness with which they affect us, stem perhaps from the fact that these customs are very much closer to our own than they appear and present us with an enigmatic image which needs deciphering. In any case this is what seems to be shown by a comparison of the facts just analysed with some features of the Tiwi naming systems which were provisionally left on one side.

It will be remembered that the Tiwi have an inordinate consumption of names: first, because each person has several names; secondly, because all the names have to be distinct; thirdly, because every re-marriage (and we have seen that they are frequent) involves giving new names to all the children a woman already has; and finally, because a person's death results in a prohibition not only of the names he has borne but also of all those which he may have been led to bestow in the course of this life. How, one may ask, do the Tiwi constantly manage to fabricate new names in these circumstances?

Several cases have to be distinguished. A proper name can be put back into circulation by the son of the deceased if he decides to take it after the period during which its use is forbidden. Many names are thus put in reserve and constitute a sort of onomastic fund which can be drawn on at will. Nevertheless, if one assumes a constant rate of births and deaths, the pool is likely to diminish on account of the prolonged duration of the taboo, unless a sudden demographic disequilibrium should act as a compensating factor. The system must therefore have other procedures at its disposal.

The chief of these, and there are in fact several, stems from extending to common nouns the prohibition on proper names when it is noticed that the two are phonetically similar. These common nouns, which are withdrawn from circulation in daily life, are not however entirely destroyed: they pass into the sacred language, reserved for ritual, where they progressively lose their meaning, the sacred language being by definition incomprehensible to the uninitiated and partly freed of any meaningful function so far as the initiated themselves are concerned. Now, sacred words, which have lost their sense, can be used to construct proper names by the addition of a suffix. Thus the word *matirandijingli* from sacred language, the meaning of which is obscure, turns into the proper name *Materandjingimirli*. This procedure is systematically employed and it has been possible to say that the sacred language is mainly composed of words which have become taboo, *Pukimani* on account of the contamination of ordinary language by the prohibition attaching to the names of the dead. Sacred language is itself exempt from this contamination (Hart).

These facts are important from two points of view. In the first place, it is clear that this complicated system is perfectly coherent: proper names contaminate common nouns; common nouns, banished from ordinary language, pass into sacred language, which in turn allows the formation of proper names. This cyclical movement is, as it were, sustained by a double pulsation: proper names origin ally lacking in meaning acquire one by being attached to common nouns and the latter relinquish their meaning on passing into the sacred language, which allows them to become proper names again. The system thus functions by pumping semantic charge alternately from common nouns to proper names and from the profane language to the sacred language. In the last analysis, the energy consumed derives from ordinary language, which coins new words for the needs of communication in proportion as the old words are taken from it. This example is an admirable demonstration of the subsidiary nature of the interpretations proposed, whether by ethnologists or by the native, to explain the prohibition on the names of the dead. For a system as well adjusted as this could not have been born of a fear of ghosts. Rather, the latter has come to be grafted on to it.

Even if one defines it, on the most general level, as consisting in an exchange of words between the profane and the sacred language, through the medium of proper names, the Tiwi system clarifies phenomena which minor aspects of our culture allowed us only to do so much as broach. We are better able to understand how terms like *Brassica rapa* which belong to a language 'sacred' in two respects (being Latin and scientific) can have the character of proper names, not, as Gardiner suggests and Hart seems prepared to admit, because they are devoid of meaning but because, in spite of appearances, they are part of a whole system in which meaning is never entirely lost. Were this not so, the sacred language of the Tiwi would not be a language but a conglomeration of oral gestures. There can, however, be no doubt that even an obscure sacred language retains potential meaning. I shall come back to this aspect of the question later.

For the moment we must distinguish another type of 'sacred' language which we employ, in the manner of the Tiwi, to introduce proper names into ordinary language, even transforming the common nouns from the domain in question into proper names. Thus, as we have already seen, we use flower names as proper names for girls, but we do not stop at this, since the inventiveness of horticulturalists provides newly introduced flowers with proper names taken over from human beings. This chassé-croisé has some notable peculiarities. The names we take from flowers and give (mainly to persons of the female sex) are common nouns belonging to ordinary language (a girl may perhaps be called Rosa but definitely not *Rosa centifolia*); those we give them in return, however, come from a 'sacred' language: a title is added to the patronym or christian name and lends it a mysterious dignity. A new flower is not usually called 'Elizabeth', 'Doumer', or 'Brigitte' but 'Queen-Elizabeth', 'President-Paul-Doumer', 'Madame-Brigitte-Bardot'. Moreover, no account is taken of the bearer's sex (in this case the grammatical gender of the name of the flower) in naming it: a rose or a gladiolus (feminine and masculine respectively in French) can be given either a man's or a woman's name indifferently. This recalls one of the rules for the attribution of 'umbilical' names among the Wik Munkan.

Now, these usages, whether also taken from our own culture or from that of Australian islanders, clearly derive from the same group as all those we have been considering; we observe the same equivalence between metonymical and metaphorical relations which has seemed to play the part of common denominator between them from the start. The names we take over from flowers to make into proper names have the force of metaphors: fair as a rose, modest as a violet, etc. But the names drawn from 'sacred' language which flowers receive in exchange have the force of metonymy, in two ways: *Brassica rapa* removes the self-sufficiency of cabbage-turnip to make it a species of a genus, part of a whole. The name 'Impératrice-Eugénie', given to a new variety of flower, performs a converse transformation, since it takes place at the level of the signifying instead of at that of the signified: this time the flower is designated *by means of* part of a whole; not any Eugénie but a particular Eugénie; Eugénie de Montijo not before her marriage but after it; not a biological individual but a person in a determined social role, etc. One type of 'sacred' name is thus 'metonymizing' and the other 'metonymized', and this opposition holds in the case examined above. It will be remembered that, as well as taking names from flowers, human beings give certain of their names to birds. These names are also 'metonymizing' for they most commonly consist of diminutives drawn from the popular language and treat the community of birds (inversely to that of flowers) as equivalent, as a whole, to a humble and well-behaved sub-group of human society. Similarly, it will readily be agreed that the metaphorical names given to dogs and cattle place the role of the figure of speech at the level of the signifying and the signified respectively.

Systematic as the set of naming procedures we have reviewed may seem, they nevertheless raise a problem. These equivalent procedures, connected with each other by relations of transformation, operate at different levels of generality. The human christian names given to birds apply to any member of a determinate species: any magpie is called 'Margot'. But the names given to flowers: Queen-Elizabeth, Imperatrice-Eugénie, etc., cover no more than the variety or sub-variety. The field of application of the names given to dogs and cattle is even more restricted. The animal's owner intends them to refer to a single individual, even though in fact each can be borne by several: there is not just one dog called 'Médor'. Only the names of racehorses and other pedigree animals are absolutely individualized. No other trotting horse than the one already so christened can be called Orvietan III in the twenty-six years of the alphabetical cycle.

This is, however, in my view, the clearest proof one could wish for that proper names and species names form part of the same group so that there is no fundamental difference between the two types of name. Or rather the reason for the difference lies not in their linguistic nature but in the way in which each culture divides up reality and in the variable limits it assigns to the enterprise of classification, depending on the problems it raises (which can differ for each particular group within the total society). It is thus by virtue of an extrinsic determination that a certain level of classification requires appellations, which can be common nouns or proper names according to the circumstances. But this does not, however, bring us back to the Durkheimian thesis of the social origin of logical thought. Although there is undoubtedly a dialectical relation between the social structure and systems of categories, the latter are not an effect or result of the former: each, at the cost of laborious mutual adjustments, translates certain historical and local modalities of the relations between man and the world, which form their common substratum.

These clarifications were necessary to enable us to emphasize, without risk of misunderstanding, the sociological and at the same time relative nature of the notion of a species as well as of an individual. From the biological point of view, men who belong to the same race (assuming that a precise sense can be given to this term) are comparable to the individual flowers which blossom, open and wither on the same tree: they are so many specimens of a variety or sub-variety. Similarly, all the members of the species *Homo sapiens* are logically comparable to the members of any other animal or plant species. However, social life effects a strange transformation in this system, for it encourages each biological individual to develop a personality; and this is a notion no longer recalling specimens within a variety but rather types of varieties or of species, probably not found in nature (although there is a suggestion of it now and again in the tropical environment) and which could be termed 'mono-individual'. What disappears with the death of a personality is a synthesis of ideas and modes of behaviour as exclusive and irreplaceable as the one a floral species develops out of the simple chemical substances common to all species. When the loss of someone dear to us or of some public personage such as a politician or writer or artist moves us, we suffer much the same sense of irreparable privation that we should experience were *Rosa centifolia* to become extinct and its scent to disappear for ever. From this point of view it seems not untrue to say that some modes of classing, arbitrarily isolated under the title of totemism, are universally employed: among ourselves this 'totemism' has merely been humanized. Everything takes place as if in our civilization every individual's own personality were his totem: it is the signifier of his signified being.

In so far as they derive from a paradigmatic set, proper names thus form the fringe of a general system of classification: they are both its extension and its limit. When they come on to the stage the curtain rises for the last act of the logical performance. But the length of the play and the number of acts are a matter of the civilization, not of the language. The more or less 'proper' nature of names is not intrinsically determinable nor can it be discovered just by comparing them with the other words in the language. It depends on the point at which a society declares its work of classifying to be complete. To say that a name is perceived as a proper name is to say that it is assigned to a level beyond which no classification is requisite, not absolutely but within a determinate cultural system. Proper names always remain on the margin of classification.

In every system, therefore, proper names represent the *quanta of signification* below which one no longer does anything but point. This brings us to the root of the parallel mistakes committed by Peirce and by Russell, the former in defining proper names as 'indices' and the latter in believing that he had discovered the logical model of proper names in demonstrative pronouns. This amounts in effect to allowing that the act of naming belongs to a continuum in which there is an imperceptible passage from the act of signifying to that of pointing. I hope that I have succeeded in showing that this passage is in fact discontinuous although each culture fixes its thresholds differently. The natural sciences put theirs on the level of species, varieties or subvarieties as the case may be. So terms of different degrees of generality will be regarded each time as proper names. The same mental operation is involved when the native sage—and sometimes scientist—also practising these modes of classification, extends them to individual members of the social group or, more precisely, to the single positions which individuals—each constituting a sub-class—can occupy at the same time or successively. From a formal point of view there is thus no fundamental difference between the zoologist or the botanist who allots a recently discovered plant the position *Elephantopus spicatus* Aubl., arranged for it by the system (if it has not indeed already been written into it), and the Omah priest who defines the social paradigms of a new member of the group by conferring the available name *Old-bison's-used-hoof* on him. They know what they are doing in both cases.

ERIS

265 Riverside Dr.
New York, NY 10025

From *The Savage Mind* by Claude Lévi-Strauss. Originally published as *La Pensée sauvage* (Paris: Librairie Plon, 1962). first published in English by Weidenfeld and Nicolson, London, 1966

Cover art: Anna Walsh, *The Spot Set*

ISBN 978-1-971559-30-8

eris.press